Contents

Authors and Acknowledgements

Susanna Whatman was born in 1752 and brought up in Stapleford Abbots in Essex. In 1776 she married James Whatman, an eminent papermaker, and moved to Turkey Court in Kent. The following year, she began to compile her housekeeping book to instruct her servants.

Thomas Balston (1883–1967) was an author, art historian and partner in the publishing house of Duckworth's. His fine collection of Victorian Staffordshire figures, which he left to the National Trust, are on show at the Bantock House Museum in Wolverhampton.

Christina Hardyment is an author, journalist and broadcaster. Her books include *Behind the Scenes: Domestic Arrangements in Historic Houses* and *Literary Trails: Writers in their Landscapes*, both published by the National Trust.

Acknowledgements
I am heavily indebted to the researches of Thomas Balston, who edited Susanna Whatman's notebooks and wrote an excellent introduction to the original edition. I have simply integrated his biographical material with my own contribution of setting the book in the context of the housekeeping advice before and since, and providing a glossary. I must also thank Professor Alistair Robb-Smith for his generosity with his original research on Hannah Glasse. Lastly, a personal thank you to Sarah Dancy and to Margaret Willes for their encouragement, advice and constructive criticism.

Christina Hardyment

THE HOUSEKEEPING BOOK

OF

SUSANNA WHATMAN
1776–1800

Introduced by
CHRISTINA HARDYMENT

Wood Engravings by
FRANK MARTIN

THE NATIONAL TRUST

First published in 1776

This edition first published in 2000 by National Trust Enterprises Limited, 36 Queen Anne's Gate, London SW1H 9AS

Reprinted 2002

Introduction © Christina Hardyment 1987, reissued 2000

Wood Engraving © Frank Martin 1956

http://www.org.uk/nationaltrust/bookshop

British Library Cataloguing in Publication Data
A catalogue record for this book is available from the British Library

ISBN 0 7078 0331 4

Printed and bound in Great Britain by Creative Print and Design Wales

Susanna Whatman in Context
Two Hundred Years of Advice on Housekeeping

S USANNA WHATMAN'S MANUSCRIPT *Housekeeping Book*
is a uniquely interesting survival. It bridges the
gap between the brief notes jotted down for the
management of servants by such eighteenth century ladies
as Elizabeth Purefoy of Shalstone or Lady Grisell Baillie of
Mellerstain, and such published advice as that offered by
the enterprising Hannah Glasse in her *Servant's Directory*. It
also stands close to the beginning of the long line of
housekeeping manuals that have overshadowed domestic
management more or less tyrannically ever since.

The most attractive aspect of Susanna's book is the
insight that it gives into the minutiae of early housecraft –
offering advice that is increasingly of interest as people
restore their homes in period style and wonder how people

used to run their kitchens and look after fine old furniture. The need to be specific about details reflected innovations in domestic life-styles with which untrained servants would be unfamiliar. As the glossary given on Susanna's instructions shows (pp.18–36), dealing with new furnishing materials such as mahogany, wallpaper, chintzes, stucco, and gilt demanded special skills and recipes. Valuable objets d'art had to be protected from the ignorant assaults of inexperienced maids. Even the lighting of a coal fire or the managing of a mangle had to be spelt out. Susanna bewailed 'the inconveniences of changing housemaids so often', because 'it is some time before one can make them understand these kind of things'.

Besides providing priceless information on eighteenth century housekeeping practice, Susanna's book forces one to revise quite dramatically the clichéed view of a wealthy and leisured female class who had little to do with the realities of household management. The Whatmans were not aristocrats, but they were very rich. James Whatman was in the happy position of failing by a very comfortable margin to spend his income. His annual balance sheets show outgoings of only £1,532; his income was more than £6,000 a year, of which £4,750 was drawn from his mills. The portrait of Susanna which George Romney finished in 1782 shows a grande dame, not a household drudge, yet Susanna clearly felt it was her business to make her maids understand the finer points of caring for a house. Susanna herself was Anglo-French, descended from a Huguenot family who had fled to England after the revocation of the Edict of Nantes in 1685. Her father, Jacob Bosanquet, was a Turkey merchant and banker, and she was brought up in the Essex manor house of Albyns, in the parish of Stapleford Abbots. As the eldest of six daughters, and having lost her mother at the age of fifteen, she became experienced in household management at an early age.

Introduction

In 1776, when she was twenty-four, she married James Whatman, an eminent English papermaker, and moved to his home in Kent. Turkey Court, and the paper mills that had made Whatman's fortune were enthusiastically described by Charles Seymour in his *Topographical Survey of Kent*, published in the very year of the Whatmans' marriage.

About half a mile from the town [Maidstone] is an elegant house, with a pretty rural scene, diversified by a perpetual verdure and the clearest streams; it exhibits at once all the happy enjoyments derived from opulent industry. This is the Mill of James Whatman, Esq., the most curious and compleat in the Kingdom.

James Whatman had by then made substantial improvements to the original three-storied red-brick William and Mary house. Just before he became High Sheriff of Kent in 1766, he had added a two-storied wing with a lofty reception room on each floor. This balanced the adjoining buildings of Turkey Mill, built by Whatman's father in 1740. In the open space between the wings, flowed the fountains and streams of the Jet d'Eau Court. William Hickey, drifting down the Thames with titled companions on a stately barge, described the hospitality offered at Turkey Court as 'princely'.

Early in the morning of the 25th [April 1768] arrived at Maidstone and here we spent five days very agreeably, our headquarters being Mr Watman's, a great manufacturer, who entertained us in a princely style. His mills and extensive works were a source of amusement to us several hours of each day, every one of our party making (awkwardly enough) a sheet of paper. In the evenings little dances and parties of the most select kind filled up the time to the hour of bed, never later than twelve. Early on the morning of the 30th we once more went on board the *Lovely Mary*, leaving the good-humoured and unostentatious hospitality of Maidstone with much regret.

The Housekeeping Book

The household at Turkey Court, where the Whatmans lived for the first eleven years of their marriage, consisted of James, his two daughters by his first marriage, Camilla and Laetitia (aged five and two in 1776), and a seventeen-year-old apprentice, William Balston, who was to become Steward in later years. Nine months after their marriage, Susanna gave birth to her only child, James, and a year later in 1778 a governess, Miss Duboulay, was employed for the benefit of the two little girls. She was succeeded by another French demoiselle, Miss Courvoisier, in 1781.

In 1782 James Whatman bought Vinters, a very ancient manor house with 86 acres of land adjoining the Turkey Mill estate. Two years later he bought another 42 acres of farmland and another paper factory, Poll Mill, from the Earl of Aylesford. All this, together with some smaller parcels of land, cost him £7,423. Six years later, after major alterations and improvements to the house, the family moved in, and Susanna had to manage a household on a rather grander scale. Her staff, oddly enough, was only increased by one servant, but she also acquired the important figure of a housekeeper, Hester Davis, who stayed with her for many years.

One of the reasons that Susanna decided to write down the necessary household routines in such detail was that under servants were much more flighty in their comings and goings than the respectable first echelon of housekeeper, steward and governess. Of the six maids employed by Susanna in 1778, two at the most remained in 1779, and of their successors two, possibly four, had gone by 1780. This was not a reflection on Susanna, who was clearly a thoughtful mistress, judging by the nice little detail in one of the later letters over the choice of a calico for the maids' dresses: 'It is a finer one than I should have given them, but it is *so pretty* that if they *fell in love* with it as I did, I should be tempted to take it'.

4

Introduction

The problem was that in the late eighteenth century good servants were at a premium, and could pick and choose their places as they wished. As the middle classes flourished on the profits of empire and industry, and began to employ more staff and live in greater style, the aristocracy felt called upon to keep larger retinues. Moreover, the best traditional source of servants, the relatively well-educated surplus sons and daughters of yeoman farmers, began to dry up as small farms were enclosed by the great landlords. A pamphleteer in 1766 pointed out that the small farms had been 'nurseries for breeding up virtuous young men and women', producing servant girls who had 'had the opportunities of learning at home how to brew, bake, cook, knit, sew, get up linen, etc, whereas poor people's children have not such advantages'.

Thieving, absenteeism, drunkenness and unexpected pregnancies appear to have been common problems below stairs. 'Dear Sally', wrote Elizabeth Purefoy in the 1740s, ''Tis not my dairymaid that is with child but my cookmaid, and it is reported our parson's maid is also with kinchen by the same person who has gone off and showed them a pair of heels for it'. After her new maid was 'apprehended for taking and conveying away strong beer out of the cellar', the harassed mistress wrote around her friends inquiring for a maid 'not possessed of too great an assurance . . . I shall like her the better if she was forty years old'.

This combination of more demanding housework and less competent servants was reflected in the precision of Susanna's notebooks compared with Lady Grisell Baillie's vague aphorisms – 'if things are alowed to run into dirt and confution, double the time and pains will not set it right, and everything that stands in dirty places will soon grow musty and stinking and unfit to be used' (1743) – or the terse instructions contained in Elizabeth Purefoy's notes on the 'Hiring of Servants and their Particular Business' (1753).

The Housekeeping Book

The Cook Maid
To roast and boil butcher's meat and all manner of fowls
To clean all the rooms below stairs
To make the servants beds and to clean all the garrets
To clean the great and little stairs
To scour the pewter and brass
To help wash, soap and buck
Or to do anything she is ordered
If she has never had the smallpox to sign a paper to leave the
service if she has them

Although there were a great many volumes in print in the eighteenth century which called themselves housekeeping manuals, on closer inspection it becomes apparent that what we now understand by the duties of a housewife and how the authors of these books saw them are two quite different things. The sub-title of Gervase Markham's 1613 *Country Contentments* conveys the fuller role of his 'English Housewife' perfectly:

> . . . Containing the inwards and outwards vertues which ought to be in a compleat woman. As, her skill in Physick, chirogery, cookery, extraction of oils, banquetting stuff, ordering of great feasts, preserving of all sorts of wines, conceited secret distillation of perfumes, ordering of wool, hemp, or flax, making cloth and dying; the knowledge of dairies, the office of malting of oats, their excellent uses in families, of brewing and baking, and all other things belonging to a household.

The pre-industrial rural home was a centre of production, not of consumption. Women were too busy spinning, baking, making soap or candles, and dealing with poultry-yard and dairy to spend much time on maintaining the outward show of immaculate order which is demanded by modern 'Good Housekeeping' standards. Even in noble households an annual turn-out was preferable to daily chores; a wash once a month or even less frequently was not unusual. Eliza Smith's *Compleat Housewife* (1736) and

Introduction

Elizabeth Raffald's *Experienced English Housewife* (1781) give a few receipts for removing mould from linen or coping with rickets, but offer no such regular plan of domestic campaign as that mapped out by Susanna. Despite their titles, both books are pre-eminently cookery books. Nicolas Chomel's *Family Dictionary* (1725) and Richard Bradley's *Country Housewife* (1727) show how undifferentiated home and garden used to be. Addressed equally to husband and wife, they talk indiscriminately of beekeeping and baking, farriers and frumenty. Some skills were certainly the wife or the husband's speciality – others were shared. A contemporary proverb ran:

Good husband without, 'tis needful there be;
Good housewife within, is as needful as he

There was a similar flexibility in the roles of servants, male and female. Maids helped out on the farm in harvest time; labourers lent a hand with spring-cleaning and the monthly wash – Susanna refers to the 'odd man' helping with mangling. William Ellis' *Country Housewife's Family Companion* (1750) again concentrates on food, mainly home-produced. It also has a section on herbal remedies, as medicine was very much a household concern. Such books read more like guides to maintaining small holdings than what we think of as housekeeping manuals; their descendants are books like John Seymour's *Self Sufficiency* rather than Mrs Beeton. The brevity of their instructions on housework are a reflection of the minor role such chores occupied in the mistress of the house's daily agenda.

Surviving copies of printed directions about the running of the house itself are remarkably rare. This may have been because so few servants could read that it was not worth printing large editions, or because what books were printed soon fell apart in use, and were thrown away rather than being preserved in state on the shelves of a gentleman's library. It is also likely that in the eighteenth century personal notebooks were probably more useful than volumes of generalised hints. But one literary curiosity survives to suggest that small books or pamphlets offering advice to servants were a familiar enough idea, whether they were the manuscript notebooks of individual housekeepers, or the printed directions of respectable tradeswomen and ex-housekeepers. Jonathan Swift's satirical *Directions to Servants* was published in 1745, and is a mad Looking-Glass version of Susanna Whatman or Hannah Glasse.

> Always keep a large fire in the kitchen when there is a small dinner or the family dines abroad . . . When you find you cannot get the dinner ready in time, put the clock back, and then it may be ready in a minute . . . It is ill housewifery to foul your kitchen rubbers with wiping the bottoms of the dishes you send up, since the tablecloth will do as well . . .
>
> When you have scoured the irons and the brasses in the parlour chimney, lay the foul wet cloth upon the next chair, that your lady may see you have not neglected your work; observe the same rule when you clean the brass locks, only with this addition, to leave the marks of your fingers on the doors . . .
>
> If you singe the linen with the iron, rub the place with flour, chalk or white powder, and if nothing will do, wash it so long till it be torn to rags . . .
>
> Fatigue of making butter: put scalding water into your churn, though in summer, and churn close to the kitchen fire, with cream if a week old. Keep cream for your sweetheart . . .

Undoubtedly the best printed book of advice by a contemporary of Susanna Whatman was Hannah Glasse's *Servant's Directory, or Housekeeper's Companion*, published in 1760. Hannah, an illegitimate by-blow of the distinguished Northumberland family of Allgood, was a London dressmaker who numbered among her clients the Dowager Princess of Wales herself. Princess Augusta's payments to her are still neatly recorded in the Hanoverian account books

Introduction

of the day. Unfortunately, most of her customers were less prompt in paying their bills, and Hannah was soon casting about for other means of earning her living. Her famous *Art of Cookery made Plain and Easy* had been published very successfully in 1747. It was aimed, as she declared in the preface, at servants: 'If I have not wrote in the high, polite Stile, I hope I shall be forgiven; for my intention is to instruct the lower Sort'. Significantly, in her preface she declared that she would not 'take it upon me to direct a Lady in the Œconomy of her Family, for every Mistress does, or at least ought to know what is most proper to be done there; therefore I shall not fill my book with a great deal of Nonsense of that Kind, which I am very well assur'd none will have regard to.'

Her assessment of the situation had changed by 1760. The *Servant's Directory or Housekeeper's Companion* was aimed at newly-weds and young house-keepers, and is full of 'Nonsense of that Kind', although the fact is tactfully veiled by Hannah's denial that she could teach 'the old experienced House-keeper' anything, and her hope that 'the young Servant will find everything necessary in regard to Household Affairs, and the Mistress saved a great deal of Trouble in teaching them'. The book is extremely detailed, particularly over the chores of the House-maid. Hannah assumes that the Laundry-maid will not need special instruction since 'she is generally brought up to it from her youth'.

A hint of the limitations of printed manuals of advice at this period is conveyed by Hannah's note at the end of a long list of different ways of cleaning linen: 'NB The reason of giving such a variety of Receipts is, this Book may go to different Places, and a Thing may be got in one Place that cannot in another'. This also explains the number of variorum recipes offered by cookery books at the period: it was not a question of a cook selecting the recipe she thought best, but a matter of using the available materials. Extreme local differences and limited transport made the idea of publishing universally applicable rules of domestic management unrealistic as well as presumptuous. Swift's satire also suggests that servants honoured such advice more in the breach than in the observance. Only when the population was so mobile that young wives would be setting up home in unfamiliar circumstances, without the traditions of their family to guide them, would there be a considerable demand for the detailed and authoritative domestic manuals of the mid-nineteenth century.

In the preface to his own *Domestic Encyclopædia* (1802), A. F. M. Willich spoke disparagingly of the 'rapid succession of Cyclopædias and Encyclopædias' which have appeared within the last twenty years, 'often more distinguished by their alluring title pages than by their intrinsic merit'. Their numbers were a reflection of the spread of literacy and the improved printing techniques at the end of the eighteenth century, which led to a massive accumulation and dissemination of knowledge in all disciplines. Dictionaries of Œconomy and Family Encyclopædias covered every domestic topic under the sun. Willich's book was informative rather than prescriptive, although he had strong opinions on hot baths ('no provident person would have recourse to a hot bath without medical advice') and the 'noxious effects' of night-air.

Mrs Parkes' *Domestic Duties* (1825) moved into a different idiom altogether: the book explicitly addressed to the mistress of the house rather than the servants. Written in the form of a conversation between two ladies, Mrs L and Mrs B, one much more experienced in household matters than the other, it recreated in print the tradition of handing down domestic expertise by the spoken word. As well as 'discussing' the best way of cleaning floors, the book takes on larger issues, such as the furnishing of the drawing-

Introduction

room, kitchen equipment, and the vexed question of whether to launder at home or send out. The courteous dialogue between social equals effectively finesses the sensitive issue of preaching to the mistress of the house, still an unacceptable approach at a time when she was assumed to be a genuine decision-maker who followed her own judgement, picking and choosing from the information offered to her. To the wise Mrs B, the ideal housekeeping manual is still the personal volume compiled by the mistress herself:

> **Mrs B:** Have you provided yourself with a cookery book?
>
> **Mrs L:** Certainly. I have purchased Mrs Rundle's and the *Cook's Oracle*. How could I go on for one day without them? Yet my study of these important books is not always satisfactory, nor are the effects produced from them at all equal to my expectations . . .
>
> **Mrs. B:** . . . As it is not always well to follow these receipt books implicitly, I recommend you to form one for yourself, of such receipts as you have found expedient to modify, and which may be done advantageously, as your own experience shall prove to you. I like to have a book of this kind at hand, in which I can insert any useful hints I may occasionally gather in conversing with others, or by my own observations . . . Besides receipts and directions in household affairs, such a book may contain many useful hints and remarks respecting that part of the management of an invalid that does not belong to a medical attendant . . .

In the *Domestic Cookery*, referred to above, Mrs Rundell remarked on the neglect of the old domestic skills in favour of drawing-room accomplishments such as piano-playing, singing, and water-colouring: 'There was a time when ladies knew nothing beyond their own family concerns; but in the present day there are many who know nothing *about* them.' The nineteenth century was the age of the parvenu, the nouveau riche who needed to be educated in the ways of their new position. As the cities grew, and industries took away manufactures from the home, housewives were no longer concerned with their dairies and still-rooms, but with settling accounts with tradesmen and paying calls. And with a new occupation, which traditionalists like Mrs Parkes regarded as quite pernicious: 'This ranging from shop to shop has also given origin to a fashionable method of killing time, which is well-known by the term *shopping*, and is literally a mean and unwarrantable amusement.'

Novel-reading was another much decried pastime of young ladies, but it threw up an attractive oddity in Margaret Dods' 1826 manual of cookery and housewifery. Written in the style of a Thomas Love Peacock novel, it was full of philosophical dialogues between 'the Cleikum Nabob' and the epicurean Doctor Redgill on the right and wrong ways of managing domestic affairs. In her preface, Mrs Dods explains that this 'novel attempt to conciliate the lovers of what is called "light reading" is intended to gain their attention to that which they may consider a vulgar and unimportant art'.

Manuals later in the century took it for granted that they would know far more than their readers, and that their readers would be eager to learn. They also increasingly conveyed an ideal domestic life-style, one of carefully calculated social display piously festooned with Christian duty. The book which completely dominated housewives in the second half of the century, and sits on many kitchen shelves to this day, was Mrs Beeton's legendary *Household Management*. In his brilliant study of turn of the century married life, *Duet, with an occasional Chorus*, Sir Arthur Conan Doyle makes his heroine declare that 'Mrs Beeton must have been the greatest housekeeper in the world. Therefore Mr Beeton must have been the happiest and most comfortable man'. Ironically, Mrs Beeton died rather young, only eight years after the publication of her book.

Originally merely a collection of articles written for her

Introduction

husband's publication, the *Englishwoman's Domestic Magazine*, it was brought up to obligatory wedding present status by the publishers Ward Lock, and swelled from the relatively slim volume of 1861 to an obese 80,000 square inches of closely packed information in 1909. Besides offering recipes on everything from 'no. 1: Bone Stock' to 'no. 3945: to Truss a Rabbit', it dealt with the daily duties of mistress and servants, entertaining guests, running the nursery and the sick room, organising accounts; even drawing up a will. It gave specifications for equipping every household, from Any Mansion, through A Good Class Home and A Middle Class Home, down to A Very Small House. By 1909 it commended Ash's Self-Filtering Refrigerator, the Grand Rapids carpet sweeper, the Villa washing-machine and the Spong tinned meat mincer: the advance-guard of the sophisticated domestic machinery now taken so much for granted in running the home.

Household Management's success reflected the fever for knowledge and direction which gripped new housewives in an age of rapid social and technological change. The tone of the volume was set by its opening words: 'The functions of the Mistress of the House resemble those of the general of an army or the manager of a great business concern.' Each servant's day was to be as precisely planned as a child's school timetable; there was a place for everything, and everything was unequivocably in its place. The next paragraph dispensed with feminists, quoting the Vicar of Wakefield to some effect: 'The modest virgin, the prudent wife, and the careful matron are much more serviceable in life than petticoated philosophers, blustering heroines, or virago queans.'

Serviceable to whom, one wonders. Independent-minded women have always got short shrift from the mainstream of domestic theorists. There was one notable exception in the writings of Charlotte Perkins Gilman, who published the most original housekeeping manual of her day, *The Home, its Work and Influence*, in 1903. Observing the increasingly rapid exodus of domestic servants, she perceived the need for community co-operation with childcare, collective kitchens, and professional services right outside the home if women were actually to achieve the economic equality they claimed to want. But louder voices over-ruled her. The spirit of the age was with the mythological Mrs Beeton and such conservative pundits as Marion Harland:

> The chief end of woman is home-making. After all the study of her capacities and capabilities, after all the proofs she has given of her power to rule the wide empire, master the abstruse sciences and write the great book, the final conclusion of the thinker is synonymous with the earlier judgement of nature. Her first duty is to be a wife and mother and make a house. Other walks are open to her if for any reason she is unable to fulfil the purpose of her being, but in so far as the opportunity to do this is denied her, she is, in a sense, a FAILURE.
>
> (*Modern Home Life*, 1902)

But what was the housewife to do about the disappearance of domestic servants? Now that alternative jobs for women were available in offices, schools, and light industry, the one-time mistress of the household increasingly often found herself being the rest of the army as well as the chief-of-staff. Once small electric motors became available in the 1920s, the rapid development of domestic technology filled housewives with optimism at the prospect of replacing their inefficient maids with 'mechanical servants'. They decided to become 'scientific managers' along the lines recommended by Christine Frederick in her articles on 'Housekeeping with Efficiency':

> Didn't I, with hundreds of other women, stoop unnecessarily over kitchen tables, sinks and ironing boards . . .? For years I never realised that I actually made 80 wrong motions in dish-

Introduction

washing alone, not counting others in the sorting, wiping and laying away.

(Ladies Home Journal, 1913)

The servantless household, she continued, offered the only opportunity for a family to follow 'exact standards'; it encouraged family co-operation and offered a chance for training children. Dozens of books selling the idea of 'servant-free' housekeeping were sold in the years between the Wars, and they offer retrospectively hilarious evidence of struggles to maintain appearances over such matters as polishing brass and answering doorbells. Housewives were advised to simplify their lives, even occasionally to ask their husbands to perform small errands. But the major responsibility for the home still rested squarely on their shoulders, and most theorists welcomed the burden:

> There is a great discipline in the performance of manifold modest daily tasks, cheered by the idea of procuring much happiness with small means for her family; to prepare food and raiment for the household, like the virtuous woman in the book of proverbs, sharpens the intelligence and warms the heart. Health too will gain by this system; we shall hear less of breakdowns and neurasthenia and of rest cures, and the nerve specialist may have to put up his shutters. Simple pleasures will in time be revived and artificiality may be doomed; the higher a woman's education, the better housewife she is sure to be.
>
> (Lily Frazer, First Aid to the Servantless, 1913)

Olive Schreiner put her finger much more accurately on the heart of the matter. In modern civilized conditions an 'unduly excessive share of labour' had evolved on the male – women had been deprived of their 'ancient domain of productive and social labour'.

> Our spinning wheels are all broken . . . Our hoes and our grindstones passed from us long ago . . . The history of our household drinks we know no longer . . . Day by day machine-

The Housekeeping Book

prepared and factory-produced viands take a larger and larger place in the dietary of rich and poor, till the working man's wife places before her household little that is of her own preparation . . . The army of rosy milkmaids has passed away for ever, to give place to the cream-separator and the largely male and machinery manipulated butter pat.

(Woman and Labour, 1911)

Although better and better machines have become available to take the drudgery out of housework since the Second World War, and dozens of manuals and magazines were published to cheer women on along the road to Wembley and the annual Ideal Home Exhibition, the general attitude to the once glorified 'profession' of housewife has become distinctly jaundiced. The challenge of Christian Duty is unfashionable – drudgery is no longer divine. Betty Freidan's best-seller, *The Feminine Mystique* (1963), put into words what millions of women are feeling: that housework is no longer a fulfilling job, that it 'expands to fit the time available', that women need more in their lives than mooning around supermarkets and refining on already adequate 'designs for living'. Although some housekeeping manuals still toe the dinner party line, an increasing number of recent publications have a rebellious tone – titles include *The I Hate to Housekeep Book*, *The Awful Brides' Book*, *How to Cheat at Housework*, and *A Life of Your Own*. Most famous of all is Shirley Conran's *Superwoman*, with its fighting motto 'Life is too short to stuff a mushroom.'

The majority of married women now have at least part-time jobs outside the home. Audrey Slaughter's *Working Wife's Handbook* deals with housework in only seven of its 250 pages. Interestingly, such books as these parallel eighteenth century texts like *The Country Wife's Companion* in the relative importance they give to housekeeping. We seem to have come full circle in two hundred years, to have substituted jobs in the market-place for the still-rooms and the dairies that kept Susanna Whatman's contemporaries so busily and productively occupied at home. Perhaps now we need no more advice on the management of our homes than a few personal notes jotted down in just such a little notebook as that kept by Susanna Whatman herself. Or, if we are lucky enough to be responsible for such valuable period pieces as Susanna cherished so wisely, the National Trust has distilled the accumulated wisdom of its own army of experienced staff in a modern *Manual of Housekeeping* that is quite unique in its good sense and expertise.

Glossary

The House Maid and Chambermaid

BEDS (p.51)   Feather beds had to be 'always well shook' and aired against dampness. 'A great evil attendant on new feathers is a disagreeable smell,' remarked Mrs Parkes (1825), 'owing to the feathers not having been sufficiently stoved to destroy the animal juice'. It was important to have a strong linen bed tick; 'a thin coarse one suffers the feathers to escape from it when the bed is shaken, and, in time, diminishes the bulk of the bed, in a greater degree that you would imagine.' Besides a feather bed, a bed would have either a wool or a hair mattress, a bolster, and two pillows. 'Those who like a high bed have straw palliasses under the mattrass.'

BOOKS, TO CLEAN (pp.39, 55)   The phrase 'as far as the

Glossary

wing of a goose will go' is a fine one; using the wing of a goose to dust books might not be such a happy notion. Mention is made of its use as a household implement as early as 1577, in Heresbach's *Four Books of Husbandry*: 'If anything remain, you must sweep it out with a Goose wing'. What most concerned the Whatmans seems to have been that the books be left undisturbed – either because their order would be confused or because old bindings might be damaged by careless handling. Leather bindings do need feeding, however, and the British Library approves a recipe which any chemist can make up: Wool Fat BP 7 oz, Beeswax Yellow BP 1948 half an ounce, Cedarwood Oil BPC 1949, one fluid ounce, Hexane, 11 fluid ounces.

CHAFING DISH (p.39)   Normally a supplementary cooking apparatus fired with charcoal; evidently from this usage also employed in damp rooms.

CARPETS (pp.39, 41, 55)   Some of Susanna's carpets were nailed down, but most were left loose. Until the middle of the century carpets were home-made or imported from the Near East, but new ones, such as those mentioned in the White Dressing Room, might well have come from the carpet factories established at Wilton in 1745 and at Axminster a few years later. Her suggestion that the carpets in the Library and Eating Parlour be cleaned by being turned over for a few days is phrased almost exactly as Hannah Glasse does in her *Servant's Directory*, and it is interesting that Susanna immediately cautions the servants not to wet the floor, while Hannah advises a scattering of wet sand. Possibly it was a floor of fine inlaid wooden blocks, better dry-rubbed than ever wetted. Perhaps she was just wary of damage to the carpets, as a month later she emphasises the need to avoid wetting them in case the colours ran.

DAYDO (p.39)   More commonly dado: and defined in the *Penny Encyclopaedia* of 1837 as 'the continuous pedestal . . . constructed of wood and usually about the height of a chair-back. Its present use is to protect the stucco work or paper of the walls'. This was probably the sense in which Susanna was using it, although it was later understood as the whole of the lower part of the wall when a different decorative finish was used. Wood-panelling was beginning to go out of fashion in the middle of the century. Susanna's contemporary Isaac Ware declared that 'for a noble hall, nothing is so well as stucco; for a parlour, wainscot seems properest; and for the apartments of a lady, hangings of paper, silk, tapestry and every other decoration of the kind'. Clearly the walls of some rooms in Susanna's house were stucco-finished, as she mentions the need for care in putting chairs against them in her instructions to the new housekeeper.

FIRES (pp.41, 43, 50)   Coal was still a luxury, delivered by sea from Newcastle, and not necessarily familiar to servants. Right at the end of the century John Byng wrote from Kent that 'A common cook here would not know how to manage a coal fire'. Misson, another eighteenth century traveller around Britain, included an exact description of how a coal fire was then lit: 'To make a coal fire, they put into the chimney certain iron stoves about half a foot high with a Plate of iron behind and beneath. Before and on each side are bars, placed and feathered like the wires of a cage, all of iron. This they fill with coal, small or great as they run, and in the middle they put a handful of small coal which they set fire to with a piece of linnen or paper. As soon as this small coal begins to burn they make use of the bellows, and in less than two minutes the other coal takes fire, You must blow a little longer after this till the fire is a little spread round.'

Glossary

FLOORS (pp.37, 38, 55, 56)   Wetting floors was regarded with some distrust – it might lead to damp, and there was much fear of unhealthy vapours resulting. So it tended to be reserved for the annual spring-cleaning, when the family was well out of the way. Soap was expensive, and left a whitish deposit on the boards, so Susanna recommended a mixture of fuller's earth (q.v.) and sand for wet scouring, and sand alone as a dry rub for floors. Hannah Glasse offered a delightfully fragrant method of using green herbs to clean floors: 'Take tanzy, mint and balm; first sweep the room, then strow the herbs on the floor, and with a long hard brush rub them well all over the boards till you have scrubbed the floor clean. When the boards are quite dry, sweep off the greens and with a dry rubbing brush, dry rub them well, and they will look like mahogany, of a fine brown, and never want other washing. This gives a sweet smell to the room . . . You may use fennel or any sweet herbs that are green, or what you can get; but tanzy, mint, balm, and fennel, are the best herbs.'

FLOOR CLOTH (p.38)   The ancestor of modern lino-leum, made from heavy canvas, flowered cloth, or old carpet impregnated with a drying oil, and left to harden. Used in passages and nurseries, and according to Mrs Rundle 'very expensive articles'. To clean it, she suggested 'Sweep, then wipe with a flannel; and when all dust and spots are removed, rub with a waxed flannel, and then with a dry plain one; but use little wax, and rub only enough with the latter to give a little smoothness, or it may endanger falling. Washing now and then with milk gives as beautiful a look and they are less slippery.

FULLER'S EARTH (p.37)   A fine dull-green clay, officially hydrous silicate of alumina, or earth of alum, used by fullers in the cloth-making industry and well-known for its cleaning properties. A Puritan preaching to housewives in 1670 declared that 'the blots of sin will easily be taken out by the soap of sorrow and the fuller's earth of contrition'.

FURNITURE .. passim Most of the furnishings of Turkey Court and Vinters were inherited from James Whatman's mother – he paid her £300 for what she left in the house, and there is no record of any substantial purchases made during his first marriage. Susanna clearly inspired rather different treatment – a Polkman Piano (£17) was acquired, cabinets and nursery beds (£55) and silver worth £164 to add to the 400 oz of plate we know he already possessed. A French clock was bought for 25 guineas in 1779, and Romney's portrait of Susanna (now in a Detroit collection) cost £25 in 1782. After the move to Vinters, Whatman spent about £5,000 reconstructing the old manor house on a sumptuous scale, and equipping it with new carpets in all the principal rooms, and new furniture.

GIRANDOLES (p.39) Candlesticks, often wall-brackets, and in this case probably valuable ones made of Venetian glass or crystal. Lady Breadalbane told her butler that he 'should never allow anyone but himself to place the best branch candlestick on the table. The lights should be all put first into the sockets, otherwise the branches will be broken.' Servants were notoriously rough with candlesticks. 'Some puts them on the fire to melt off the grease, by which they are burnt and unsoldered; if thrown under the grate which is the general way, they are bruised and battered to pieces'. Hannah Glasse recommended a quick dip into rapidly boiling water, even for china and japanned candlesticks, but warned that they needed great care and speedy drying.

Glossary

LOCKS (p.40)   Until the introduction of single tumbler mechanisms towards the end of the century, locks were simple affairs, little more than spring-loaded bolts activated by a key. Susanna's were clearly made of brass and might even have been the new locks with neat tubular keys invented by Joseph Bramah in 1784. Hannah Glasse recommended putting a piece of pasteboard over the lock, and cutting a hole big enough to slip it over the lock to preserve the door from any marks while it was being polished with rotten-stone or white brick, standard brass-cleaners at that time.

MAHOGANY (pp.39, 41, 56)   Mahogany, widely introduced into fine furniture making in the eighteenth century was a very highly rated wood – more resistant to worm and damp than any other. It was not to be waxed, only rubbed, as the cabinet's maker's finish was an adequate protection. A linseed oil rub was recommended by some authorities, but it darkened the wood unfashionably. A bellows was often used to blow dust from intricately carved pieces.

PAPERS . . . TOPS OF BEDS (p. 37)   Mrs Parkes is more specific: 'For the top of the bed I recommend you to have several sheets of cartridge paper pasted together, and laid upon the tester, which, as the dust accumulates upon it, can be drawn off and cleaned' (*Domestic Duties*, 1825).

PICTURES (p.38)   Hannah Glasse also warned against dusting pictures, and suggested using a bellows. She gave two methods of actually cleaning them. The first involved gentle brushing with a mixture of vitriol, borax and water, the second sponging with wood ashes. Revarnishing was either by spreading nut and linseed oil over the canvas with a feather, or gently sponging it with the froth from the top of a bowl of well beaten egg-white – 'When dry, it will look charmingly. Nor does this varnish crackle, but preserves the picture better than any thing else can do; nor can any picture-cleaner in the world clean them better'. Restorers at the National Gallery might not agree.

PILLOW BEAR (BERE) (pp.39, 53)   Old-fashioned term for a pillow case – Chaucer's charlatan Pardoner had one, 'which called he Our Lady's Veil'. Swift's *Directions to Servants* (1745) referred to pillow cases rather than bears.

TEA-LEAVES (p.39)   These have a respectable ancestry as carpet cleaners; an example of household serendipity at its best. Sand would have been far too gritty to use on carpets; tea-leaves were already damp enough to attract the dust and could be easily swept up. It also stopped the maids from indulging in the well-documented domestic chicanery of drying the used leaves and reselling them – or maybe they ended up in the poorer cottager's charpots dust and all.

VENETIAN BLINDS (pp.38, 39, 56)   Any good house-keeper knew how destructive the sun was of pictures, furnishing and hangings, and the very first advice in the modern National Trust *Manual of Housekeeping* is to keep rooms shielded from sunlight. Susanna's staff had to move round the house with the sun, putting the blinds up and down, and she is absolutely precise about the hour at which the sun gets to each room. She also mentions the covers on the furniture in the drawing-room. Great houses spent most of the time shrouded in a perpetual twilight against the twin enemies of light and dust. When Mr Sponge set off on his *Sporting Tour*, 'he had the house put away in Brown Holland, the carpets rolled up, the pictures covered, the statues shrouded in muslin'.

WATER CLOSET (p.37)   At this time only the wealthiest

families boasted of Water Closets. although a flushing pan had been designed by Queen Elizabeth's godson, Sir John Harington as early as 1596 and Queen Anne was supplied at Windsor with 'a little place of Easement of marble, with sluices to wash all down'. In the eighteenth century, closets seem to have been more common in France than in England or America, and Susanna's French upbringing may have made her something of a sanitary innovator in England. A Parisian advertisement of 1759 describes a polished oak model with gilt fittings, but no British patents at all were entered for water closets between 1617, when the Patent Office opened, and 1775: an extraordinary hiatus. It may have been that closets were constructed as a matter of course by local builders, who did not consider patents necessary to immortalise any improvements they might make. Unfortunately, this means that few details of closets made before 1775 exist. The standard mechanism of the eighteenth century, if there was a sluice at all, was the pan closet. This had an upper bowl of lead, marble, or glazed pottery. Below was a large container, with waste pipe, in which hung a hinged metal pan. When level, this formed a water-filled base to the upper bowl. By pulling a handle, it tilted down and all, or nearly all, of its contents fell into the bowl beneath. Its efficiency depended on the amount of water available to wash it out, but the lower bowl was difficult to clean and did not drain effectively.

In 1775, Alexander Cummings, a Bond Street watch-maker, invented the valve closet. This, after Joseph Bramah's modification to the original inefficient valve, was to remain popular until the end of the nineteenth century and a few survive to this day. The closet actually had two valves, one to let the water in, and one attached to the 'slider' which controlled the outlet at the bottom of the basin. The interconnection of these valves made the pan a quick and vigorous flusher, although again not always guaranteed to dispose of everything, and rather too prodigal of water to suit the water companies.

The Cook

Kitchens of grand houses in the late eighteenth century look satisfyingly simple in the frontispieces of the many contemporary books of cookery recipes. They show stone-flagged floors, high dressers loaded with platters of all sizes, windsor chairs and wide wooden tables, meat sizzling on a spit, a kettle simmering on a trivet. There were drawbacks. Freezing without the range lit, they became oppressively hot when it was blazing away to roast the several joints that constituted part of the main daily meal. A rabbit-warren of sculleries, pantries, larders and still-rooms separated the several processes of food preparation. As Susanna emphasised, method and order were vital: 'a place for everything and everything in its place'.

DRESSER CLOTHS (p.44)   See Linen below.

KITCHEN RANGE (p.43)   The Whatmans' range was probably of the type invented and described by Thomas Robinson in 1780. 'At one side of the fire is the oven and the other is made to wind up with a cheeck. The top bar in front is made to fall down occasionally to a level with the second bar. The moving cheeck is made with a socket in it to receive a swinging trivet. The oven is made of cast iron, nearly square front, the door hung with hinges and fastened with a handle and a turn-buckle and the oven is provided with fillets for the shelves to rest upon. The oven must be enclosed with bricks and mortar.'

Such a range was a great improvement on the old open fire with its chimney crane and spits. Once the daily task of cooking was over, the fire could be 'wound up' to a smaller size, just enough to keep the chill off the kitchen and the water boiler hot.

MEAT SAFES (p.45) 'Portable cupboards, generally of wood, with side and door panels made of some perforated substance to let the air on properly but to preclude the entrance of flies and insects.' (*Webster and Parkes*, 1841). In large households, when a slice off a joint was a tempting little perk, it was common practice until well into the nineteenth century to lock up the more valuable joints of meat; indeed some early twentieth century refrigerators continued the old pattern and were provided with locks.

NOONING (p.43) The noon meal. In the eighteenth century only gluttons ate more than one major meal a day. It was likely that the servants ate their main meal of the day earlier than the family, although in some old fashioned country circles, gentlemen still ate at the traditional hour of twelve. The Whatmans were near enough to London to be affected by society's new ways, and in fashionable circles dinner was becoming later and later. 'In my memory,' wrote Richard Steele, 'the dinner hour has crept from 12 o'clock to 3'. Sixty or seventy years later around five o'clock or six was usual – although Horace Walpole admitted that he was still 'so antiquated to dine at four'. Soon circles of the highest ton were delaying their meal until eight o'clock, and in the nineteenth century luncheon became a more substantial meal.

PEWTER (p.43) A typical recipe for pewter polish was made from a boiled down solution of one pail of wood-ashes and half a pail of unslaked lime mixed into four pails of soft water. This was bottled and stored. When needed it was warmed up for use, poured into two little basins of red sand, and then used first to scour and then clean the pewter.

'Set them to dry and they will look like new . . . brass and copper can be cleaned in the same way'.

POOR PEOPLE'S BROTH (p.45)   A similar custom clearly prevailed in the Breadalbane household, as one of Lady Breadalbane's directions is that 'The poor's kitchen must be kept neat and clean and regularly swept by the man who makes the broth'. Broken victuals — leftovers, rather than the scrapings of the plates which went into the hogs' pail — were not to be servants' perks but alms for the deserving poor.

SINK . . . IN THE COURT (p.40) There are several clues to the fact that the Whatmans' plumbing was more sophisticated than this suggests. One was the mention of a Water Closet, another the famed Jet d'Eau court in front of Turkey Court, a third the evidence of a Laundry room. So the sink in the yard was likely to be a secondary one, a hangover from a time when the only available water was pumped from rainwater tanks. The Scullery, where the cook was instructed to have a care that 'heavy things were not placed *upon* the plates and dishes', probably had a sink as well. James Whatman was a man of means, and it seems unlikely that he did not take advantage of the general availability — at a price — of steam and hydraulic water-raising engines. As early as 1720, Mr Fowke of Wapping was offering for sale 'Pumps, which may be work'd by one Man, for raising water out of any well, upwards of 120 feet deep, Sufficient for the Service of any private House or Family, and so constructed that by turning a Cock may supply a Cistern at the Top of the House, or a bathing Vessel in any Room'. At the same time, the care with which Susanna emphasises where water should be thrown could mean that there were no other soakaways — and her slightly apologetic

Glossary

excuses for the sink not being covered in could also mean that it was the only source of water.

SKREEN (p.44)   A mobile shelf-unit lined with tin plate which shielded the cook from the heat of the range, as well as keeping warm the numerous dishes sent up for each course at the same time.

STILIARDS (p.45)   A portable weighing scale, to be had in sizes to weigh everything from babies to railway luggage, and probably named after the beam used at the Steelyard, London base of the sixteenth century Hanseatic League's trading. It consisted of a lever with unequal arms moving on a fulcrum. The article to be weighed was hung on the shorter arm, and a counterpoise slid down the longer notched arm until an equilibrium was produced. The matter of occasionally checking the weight of meat when it was delivered is another example of the careful attention to accounting that was the hallmark of conscientious house-keeping.

The Laundry Maid
Processing laundry was a slow business in the eighteenth century, involving a heavy expenditure of time, soap and labour. Only the very poorest households did their own washing. Most people sent their clothes to a washerwoman; the gentry employed a laundry maid, and filled the time she did not need for washing with other domestic chores – helping out the housemaid, mending or spinning. A superb example of a laundry built in the late eighteenth century remains almost completely intact at the National Trust house Erddig, in North Wales.

On Monday clothes and linen would be checked for stains, soaked (or 'bucked') in a lye, a solution of wood-ash, and boiled. They were washed and hung out to dry on Tuesday, folded on Wednesday, and mangled on Thursday or Friday. Delicate garments were washed separately on Monday and ironed on a dresser or board.

IRONING (pp.48, 49)   The flat or 'sad' irons generally in use in the eighteenth century could either be heated up on a hot-plate on the kitchen range, or over a small purpose-built furnace set into a chimney breast beside it, or set at the sloping sides of a purpose-built free-standing charcoal stove. Cleaner in use were box-irons, hollow irons with a sliding back panel into which slugs of hot metal, or even glowing charcoal, could be inserted. Ruffles on shirts and frocks were best finished off on the slim cylindrical Italian irons, again hollowed out to hold metal slugs or short pokers. Purpose-built ironing boards were rare, although Susanna mentions a 'board' put up at Vinters for the Housekeeper. More usual was a piece of flannel or blanket securely pinned down on a table or dresser.

MANGLING (p.46–7)   Mangling was a smoothing process which originated in northern Europe in the sixteenth century, and was intended not only to press linen flat but to give it a shining finish. Originally the almost dry linen was spread on a wide table and wound round a large wooden roller. A heavy wooden board, about two feet long, and four or five inches wide, with a handle at each end, was placed on top of the roller and pressed down onto it, moving it up and down the table until a fine glazed finish appeared. An early improvement on this was the massive box mangle, an oblong wooden chest full of stones which was propelled over several linen-wrapped rollers by straps attached to each end of the box and passed over an upper roller carried round by a winch. 'The labour of working it is excessive', commented Webster and Parkes (1841), 'not only on account of the strength required to move it, but from the continual reversing of the motion; for scarcely has it been got into motion by great exertion, than it becomes necessary to turn it back again'.

The mangle mentioned by Susanna must have been such a box mangle because clearly at least two people were needed to operate it – 'one at each side'. It would also need to be lifted on and off the 'wide table' used for rolling. An improved machine on a stand, and worked by a handle, won George Jee a silver medal from the Society for the Advancement of Arts, Manufacturers and Commerce in 1797, but the rack and pinion mechanisms and fly-wheels which made such machines operable by a single washerwoman were not generally introduced until Baker's machines of the 1830s.

Mangling was an art. Crooked cloths or careless creasing could mar the texture of the material, and any dirt attached to the rollers or box would be literally ground into the cloth. The mangle cloths of pale brown Holland, an unbleached linen cloth, were wrapped carefully over the clothes or linen being mangled, and smaller items were protected by bags of Holland. 'Unseemly creases' had to be taken out afterwards by ironing.

SOAP (p.37)   As the animal fats and vegetable oils which went into the making of soap were also greatly in demand for cooking and candle making, soap was an expensive item, made more so by the periodic imposition of excise duties on it until 1853. James Whatman bought soap in London, but many eighteenth century housewives made their own. Benjamin Franklin recommended the recipe he was given by his sister who lived in England: 'Eighteen bushels of ashes, one bushel of stone lime, three pounds of tallow, fifteen pounds of the purest Barbary wax of a lovely green colour and a peck of salt'.

The Housekeeping Book

WOODEN BOWLS (p.51)   To prevent the wooden bowls used for washing from cracking, Hannah Glasse suggests taking them to the tallow-chandler and having them boiled with the tallow.

The Housekeeper

'The mistress of a large family can neither afford the time, nor even have it in her power, to see what her servants are about, she must depend upon the Housekeeper to see all her orders are enforced and every rule kept up'. Susanna engaged Hester Davis in 1782, when her children were eleven, eight and five years old. *The Housekeeping Book*, with its amendments and additions, was largely for Mrs Davis' benefit; perhaps she read the relevant passages out to new servant maids on their hiring. It was also for posterity, to help Susanna's daughter-in-law to understand the pattern to which the servants were accustomed.

CLOSET STOREROOM (p.52)   This and the other pantries and larders were under the personal eye of the Housekeeper. Sugar and spices were expensive, and were usually kept locked up. The *Queen's Closet Open'd* was a popular manual on the art of 'preserving, candying and cookery'; it included recipes for Melancholy Water and Candied Cowslips, Portugal Eggs (set in a sea of red jelly, and decorated with gilded laurel leaves) and Snail Water ('excellent for Consumption . . . Take a peck of snails with the shells on their backs . . .')

LINEN (pp.44, 45, 50, 52)   The grander the household, the greater the contents of the traditional 'bottom drawer' of linen which was part of a bride's dower. Ann Cook's *Plan of Housekeeping* (1760) suggests 'four webs of sheets, 44 yards each, two fine and two coarse; also a web of Diaper and one of Hugaback for tablecloths' for a modest four bedroomed house. Lady Osbaldistone of Hunmanby's storeroom boasted thirty-two tablecloths (not including those for the servants), one hundred and seventeen dinner napkins, one sideboard cloth, four 'sideboarders' [possibly equivalent to Susanna's 'dresser-cloths', p.26] and three bread cloths. Far greater quantities of bed-linen, napery, and table-cloths were necessary to establishments such as Lady Grisell's at Mellerstain, which might find themselves feeding twenty people or more a night. Counting, marking, mending, and keeping track of the linen as it circulated in use was an important part of any housekeeper's job.

SEWING (pp.49, 50)   Before the invention of the sewing machine in the 1840s, few women spent a day without a needle in their hands. Any spare time that the maids had was to be occupied in 'making and mending'.

The Dairymaid

Many women took a pride in the state of their dairy – great ladies from Marie Antoinette at the Petit Trianon to Queen Victoria at Osborne played at being dairymaids themselves. 'A pretty sight is a first-rate dairy', wrote Disraeli in *Lothair*, 'with its flooring of fanciful tiles, and its cool shrouded chambers, its stained-glass windows and its marble slabs, and porcelain pots of cream and plenteous platters of fantastically formed butter.' But Susanna's dairy was no plaything – the note-books show her to be a business woman who took a pride in efficient husbandry as well as domestic management. She also knew when sheep-shearing and haymaking would infringe on domestic tasks, and her maids spun and carded wool as well as polishing the floors and furniture.

SCOWERING (p.44)   All the vessels used in the dairy had to be kept extremely clean, for fear of tainting the milk. They were scalded and scoured with salt by the Dairymaid in the kitchen because no hot water of any kind was allowed in the dairy, for fear of the heat injuring the milk. White-finished earthenware bowls were preferred for dairy use. Lead and copper finishes were potentially poisonous, and cast-iron vessels gave a disagreeable taste to the milk.

STRIP THE COWS (p.51)   An indication that Susanna knew exactly how to milk: the final 'stripping' ensures that no milk is left undrawn.

Men about the House
The senior male employee in the Whatman household was William Balston, the Christ's Hospital apprentice who was promoted first to Steward, then chief assistant at the paper-mills, and at length, after Whatman's death, became a partner in the mills himself. Next came the Butler, who oversaw the other male servants, and was charged with the care of the cellar, the candles, and the plate. From the evidence of the Whatman account books, there were generally six or seven men on the payroll, a luxury that few people could afford after the punitive Servants' Tax levied on male servants after 1778. These included a coachman and a gardener, but the others had domestic duties. Susanna makes no reference to them, except a mention of the 'odd man' who helped with the mangling, and it seems likely that they were directly answerable to Whatman, who clearly kept a close eye on household affairs (see bills below).

ALE ALLOWANCE (p.57)   Drinking water was at a pre-mium in the eighteenth century, and one of the major tasks

Glossary

of the Housekeeper and Butler was to superintend the brewing of ale, small beer, and the various 'cordials, juleps and aromatic waters' that were to be found in the best stillrooms. Every one of Lady Grisell's servants was allowed a mutchkin (about half a litre) of beer at every meal 'except when they get milk, which is always when there is any to give them, and then they have only beer for their dinner'.

BILLS (p.53)   The Whatman account books are orderly and detailed volumes, full of revealing items. James paid sums ranging from £10 to £25 into the House Purse, and Susanna accounted to him for every penny spent. He then entered all expenses into the account books. At the end of each year he made an analysis of them under various headings, and a glance at just one year provides a fascinating insight into relative expenses of the eighteenth century 'shopping basket'. In 1781, for example, food bills amounted to £222, other household bills to £325, servants' wages and clothes to £211, and the stables' accounts to £184. Susanna received an allowance of £105, the three children's governess, clothes, etc. cost £89, and his own personal expenses amounted to £143. Evidently a 'warm man', Whatman put Micawber's petty recipe for happiness to shame: his income was over £6,000 a year, and his outgoings on all accounts only £1,532.

CANDLES (pp.51, 53, 57)   These, particularly the best quality spermaceti ones made from the fatty white substance found in the head of the sperm whale, were expensive items. 'All the pieces of spermaceti candles are to be collected by the under Butler and given over to the House-Keeper at least once a fortnight for the lanthorns and the lighting of fires' directed Lady Breadalbane. James Whatman brought Susanna's candles from London; lesser households often made their own from tallow, the hard white fat found around the kidneys and caul of animals.

PLATE (p.57)   Silver and gold dishes – solid, rather than plated with metal – were best kept locked up out of temptation's way. Much of it was antiquated and rarely used, but Mrs Parkes felt that it 'marks ancestorial dignity, and, therefore, is not likely to be despised by the generality of its possessors.' She recommended rubbing silver plate with 'a mixture of variegated hartshorn [literally, the ground horn of a deer, chief domestic source of ammonia in the eighteenth century] and turpentine' twice a week, and rubbing it with leathers daily.

Christina Hardyment 1987

The House Maid

TO USE AS LITTLE SOAP AS POSSIBLE (IF ANY) IN SCOWER-
ing rooms. Fuller's earth and fine sand preserves the
colour of the boards, and does not leave a white
appearance as soap does. All the rooms to be dry scrubbed
with white sand.

To take the papers off the tops of the beds twice a
year.

To whisk all the window curtains every Saturday. Shake
mats, carpets, etc. every Saturday. To use a painter's brush
to all the ledges, window frames and furniture, and then the
duster. Never to use a hard brush to any mahogany carving
that has been neglected and the dust suffered to settle
in it.

To keep a small mop in the cupboard in the Water

Closet, and use warm water every day to keep the inside clean. In frosty weather not to pour it too hot, only just warm. And it must be used in a mug, not in anything so wide as a bason, that it [do] not wet the sides of the pan.

To rise on Tuesday morning to wash her own things and the dusters, and help wash stockings. To iron her own things of an evening. To mend the towels and her Master's common stockings of an evening.

To work in [the] Storeroom every day after her house work is finished, except Saturday, when every thing must be looked to that wants doing weekly. Housemaid folds with the Laundrymaid every Wednesday.

To take turns of going to Church every other Sunday with the Laundrymaid.

Never to dust pictures, nor the frames of anything that has a gilt edge. Never to dust the black busts.

To force back all the window shutters: otherwise they get warped, and will not go into their place, which makes a room look very bad indeed. To sweep the steps in front of the house every morning when necessary.

When a floor cloth wants washing, not to use a brush or soapsuds, but a soft linen and some fresh milk and water. A steel should be used round the hearth and in all dirty corners.

Venetian blinds. When let down, to pull the longest string to turn or close them quite. Otherwise the sun will come through the laths.

The Housemaid must be an early riser, because the ground floor should be ready against the family come down stairs. In summer when the stoves take less time, and there is also less dust and dirt, the Housemaid should dry rub some part every morning, as the floors get sooner dirty in summer from the insects, and if they are well dry rubbed all summer, they will keep well with a very little attention in the winter, which cannot be given at that time of the year in a morning, but may occasionally when the family drive out.

All doors at places where the dust lodges should be attended to. Otherwise, if left too long, it takes a long time and much labour to get it off.

If the Housemaid perceives that any stitches are wanting in sheets or pillow bears when she puts them to the fire, she should return them to the Housekeeper, unless she chooses to mend them herself, which is not required of her. If any mending is necessary before they go to the wash, they should be taken into the storeroom.

The sun comes into the Library very early. The window on that side of the bow must have the blind let down. The painted chairs must not be knocked against anything, or against one another. A chair must not be placed against the door that goes into Mr Whatman's Dressingroom. All the space between the daydo and skirting board is plaister. Therefore, if it is knocked, it will break. The books are not to be meddled with, but they may be dusted as far as a wing of a goose will go. Nothing put behind the door besides the ladder. Tea leaves used on the carpet in this room, Drawingroom, and Eating Parlor, and Mrs Whatman's Dressingroom, no where else.

Drawingroom. The blinds always closed in the morning and window up. Kept dusted, and the chairs and sofas dusted occasionally, and the mahogany rubbed. The covers shook. The girandoles Mrs W always cleans herself. They should never be touched: nor the pictures. In damp weather a chafing dish with coals should be used, but something put under it to ketch any dirt that may fall. When the fire is light and the stove cleaned, something must be laid down to prevent the carpet from being dirtied, *as it is nailed down.* The other carpets are not.

In every room care must be taken not to open the windows with dirty hands. The locks in every room should be kept bright, the keys kept clean.

Eating Parlor. The sun never comes in. The chairs must be well dusted so that the mahogany should look bright. The carving on the mahogany sideboards should be kept free from dust with the painter['s] brush. No chair should be set in the corner near the door to the kitchin. The pianoforte and the harpsichord should not have anything struck against them. Brass rings and mahogany stands. The sideboard tables are made to move, but this can seldom be necessary, and when they are, they should be set even between the door and wall, and a hand placed behind to prevent the corners and edges breaking the stucco.

Hall and Staircase. Swept and dusted every day, and the banister occasionally rubbed with a very little oil and every day with a dry cloth.

To fold Wednesdays with the Laundrymaid.

The Housemaid and Chambermaid take it by turns every week to clean out the sink and yard in the court and the under gutter that runs the top of the Shoe House, which could not be slanted, so requires a brush along it to remove any impediments. The steps [are] kept near on purpose, and the Cook may pitch them when she wants to open her high cupboards, which is seldom. No water must be thrown down in the court instead of throwing it in the sink, because wherever the earth is kept wet, it will sink and the square stone, when it wants support, will break. When this happens the water will lodge instead of running off, and if the court is kept in damp all wet seasons, the walls of the house will suffer at the foundation. The sink would have been light by a window, and the court shut up, but a door would have been inconvenient when a ladder was required in the court.

The Laundrymaid is not to do anything in the best rooms when it is her Sunday to be at home, because the

The House Maid

Housemaid has time enough for the lower rooms if she rises early, and the furniture might suffer by a person not used to the care of it.

In lighting fires care should be taken to lay the fire properly, particularly in rooms where they are apt to smoak at first lighting. In this case cinders and round coals should be placed at bottom of the grate, then pieces of wood laid hollow, over which should be a few large cinders laid lose. By this arrangement the smoke goes upwards without impediment. The Housemaid should never fail sweeping down the sutt every morning as high as she can reach.

Always to turn up the carpet round the fire and sweep it under every day, except in summer, when twice a week, the same as the other part of the carpet, is sufficient.

Mrs Whatman's Dressingroom. The sun must always be kept out, or it will spoil the carpet, chairs and mahogany cabinet. This cabinet is of very nice workmanship and should be well rubbed occasionally, but it has acquired such a very fine polish by good care that common dusting will keep it in order. The chairs, although mahogany, are varnished. The same care must be taken not to knock them as if they were painted.

The Bedchamber. The sun must be kept out of this room, as it shines full on the bed early and on the mahogany press at one o'clock.

White Dressingroom. Care for painted chairs, and same for mahogany drawers and dressing table. Sun comes in at two o'clock.

White Bedchamber. Painted dressing table, and hansome mahogany press, and new carpets. Sun must be kept out for these and the pictures. Sun comes in at two o'clock.

North Dressingroom. Painted dressing table and mahogany press. Sun comes in at two o'clock.

North Bedchamber. The sun never comes in. All these

rooms must be kept aired, and the flies and flygoldings[1] destroyed in time.

Little Dressingroom beyond. The rain comes in a little at the casement. A servant's bed is in the inward part.

No carpet in any of the rooms should be laid nearer than the wooden edge of the hearth, unless it is lined with coarse cloth, which none of the carpets at Vinters are.

Yellow room. Common dusting, airing, and keeping clean. The sun comes in very early and is off by noon.

Mr Balston's Room. The same.

James's Room. The same.

Miss Whatmans' Bedchamber.[2] The same.

Young ladies' Dressingroom. The same.

Garretts to be kept as airy as possible, and in summer the beds swept under. If necessary, with lime water: otherwise plain water is sufficient.

Mr Whatman's Dressingroom. The sun in the east window quite shut out, and the south window whilst we are at breakfast.

The Garrets' beds hold eighteen servants. The Garrets should be swept three times a week, Mondays, Thursdays and Saturdays, Tuesday being washing morning, and Wednesday the day for foulding.

---

[1] A Kentish word for ladybirds.

[2] The MS. reads 'Miss Whatmans Bedchamber, with no apostrophe. This must be the common parlance for 'Misses Whatman's', since no other bedroom is mentioned for Camilla or Laetitia, and at that period there was no Miss Whatman (except, of course, Camilla) intimately connected with the family.

The Cook

HAVING A SERVANTS HALL SO VERY CONVENIENT AT Vinters we mean all the servants should have their nooning in it as the Kitchen is not large. In the Old Book it sais the Cook must bake her bread in the morning time enough for breakfast. She should bake Wednesdays and Saturdays, clean her Larder and Pantries Mondays and Fridays, and rise Tuesday to wash her own things. Thursday morning wipe her pewter or do any other early job, or, as a favor, she may get her kitchen business forward and iron her things instead of doing it in the evening, as sometimes late dinners etc. make it inconvenient if there is supper to be got.

To keep as little fire in the Kitchen as may be necessary, always winding up the grate after dinner. The Cook may have some large coals picked for the Kitchen whenever necessary: the Bedchambers never should.

The Cook should see that every Saucepan etc. is well cleaned within, but they should not be scowered bright without, except the upper rim.

When a new Cook comes the Housekeeper should see that she does this with the other servants by doing it herself, and then seeing it done for several following days. When a new Cook comes, much attention is necessary till she is got into all the common rules and observances such as the care above mentioned: filling the hog pails: washing up butter dish, sallad bowl, etc.: giving an eye to the scowering of saucepans by the Dairymaid: preserving the water in which the meat is boiled for broth: keeping all her places clean: managing her fire and her kitchen linen: making good bread etc. Such things are material points, and of more consequence to be *first* attended to than any part of the cookery, except the quite common attentions of cleaning the fish properly, roasting and boiling in a proper manner, warming up the servants' breakfasts.

The Cook should *see* that heavy things are not set in the Scullery *upon* the plates and dishes. She may always call back a servant whom she sees do it, or if they leave bones or hard things such as spoons etc. in a dish, and then put other dishes on it.

The Cook should have all proper kitchin linen and keep it good and mended. The Housekeeper or the Mistress should look it over every now and then. The dishes before dinner should all be set in the skreen to get hot, and the bottoms wiped that they may not dirty the table cloth. Indeed, if a dresser cloth is used, they cannot well come up soiled.

A certain order or method is necessary at dishing up, and there is no excuse for waiting for a second course, the Kitchin being so near, as the Housekeeper may always have any of the maids to assist the Cook at the going in of the dinner. This teaches the Cook to contrive, and be quicker, in case the Housekeeper is ill or absent from home.

Butter, raddishes, or anything that spoils in a hot kitchin should be placed near the parlor door, as should the cheeze, to be ready to come in.

There should be a place in the Kitchin for everything kept there, otherwise it will be lost or mislaid without being *missed*, and [this] holds good for every other department, and saves many things, and *much trouble*.

All linen should be marked according to its purpose, its

number and the year besides the name. This saves a great deal of trouble with house linen.

The meat is weighed every week when it comes in all together. The separate joints that come in singly are only weighed now and then occasionally, just to keep an eye on the regularity of the Butchers. A pair of stiliards are kept in the Kitchen for this purpose, brought up when we came to Vinters.

As the comfort of the servants is attended to, in their having always their victuals well dressed and a plenty, it is expected they should not make any waste, and all broken victuals are to be at the disposal only of the Housekeeper, and no liberty is allowed of any other servant giving anything away that is left after the Housekeeper has seen to the poor people's broth etc., which generally takes up all remains of bits of bread etc. And when there is any garden stuff that is not wanted and would otherwise be lost, it must be brought up and given from the House, as the gardiner has no liberty of giving away anything out of the garden.

As it is very wrong to lay temptation unnecessarily in the way of anyone, the large joints should not be left open to the inferior servants. There are two keys to the little wire safe, one for the Cook and one for the Housekeeper, that there may be no excuse for the leaving roast or boiled beef, legs of pork, etc. in the open safe. This duty of keeping away temptation is very necessary, as it would be difficult to detect depredations on a large joint, and a dishonest servant might contract a habit of doing injustice, and be more difficult to reclaim than when immediate detection follows.

There is a larger boiler for water, and a large tea kettle for the Kitchin fire. No more tea kettles should be put on. Davis has a small one by her particular desire for the Storeroom, but it is never to be put upon the Kitchin fire.

The Housekeeper ought always to be *present* when the dinner is sent up, even when quite alone. Otherwise the Cook is apt to relax, and be longer dishing than is necessary, or to omit her dresser cloths or getting the dishes warmed, or the sauce boats etc. The dishes should not be made too hot.

The Laundry Maid

TO LOOK OVER LINEN IN THE STOREROOM MONDAY morning, put stitches or buttons in all her Master's shirts. If more is wanting, as new risbands and collars, she is to put them by for the Housekeeper. If any table cloth wants more than a few stitches, to put it by for Housekeeper to mend the end of the week.

To rise early on Tuesday morning to wash, and the other maids also to do their own things, except the Dairymaid, who on account of her Dairy washes Monday evening. And the Cook then washes her dishes and sauce pans.

To be very careful in mangling that the mangle is wiped free from soil, that the linen is rolled quite smooth, and that the mangling cloths are even. The cloths should hardly ever be washed, because they are long in acquiring that *shining* polish which makes the linen look so well. They should be of pale brown Holland manufactured on purpose, to be had at the mangle makers.

The Laundry Maid

To take turns every Sunday at Church with the House-maid. On those days to help make beds, do the Garretts and the Bedchamber floor.

Fold on Wednesdays, mangle Thursday or Friday as may be most convenient. If the odd man is busy, the other maids may turn the mangle, one at each side. Very particular attention to the mangling is necessary, and if the House-keeper cannot give a look in any week, she should examine the linen when it comes in after the wash to see that there is nothing wrong. The mangling cloths will generally point that out. The difference between proper mangling and care-lessness makes as much difference in the look as between fine linen and coarse, and as table linen is worn round in turns, it may be a considerable time before any mischief is perceived in the Parlor. The general attention to a mangle is to see that it runs even, is carefully wiped of any dust or gritty matter, and that oil is properly supplied to the wheels, which will wear away and spoil without this atten-tion. They should sometimes be cleaned from the dirt which will mix with the oil, and have the appearance of combe.

The clothes dried out of doors when the weather permits. The table linen doubled in two, three, or four, according to its size. A wide table always used for rolling.

To begin to wash middle of day Monday the young ladies' fine and small things, ditto for the governess and the gen-tlemen's shirts and neckcloths.

The Dairymaid only washes plates and dishes, not the basons, cups, sallad bowl or tureen, egg glasses etc. These things of course fall upon the Cook.

New mangling clothes bought in 1784. The former ones did not last more than ten years because they were ill used. Mrs Mellish[1] had not had new ones for thirty years.

---

[1] Mrs Mellish cannot be traced. She appears to have bought her mangling clothes not later than 1744. She may have been Housekeeper at Turkey Court in the time of Whatman's parents.

N.B. Ours are of the wrong sort, and we must have the brown in future, as the common Irish does not at all answer for the look of the linen.

1799. We have again had new mangling cloths, and that without my being consulted, and they are again of common linen. I have spoke very seriously about it, that nothing of the kind may happen in future. The Laundrymaid is to keep her own ironing flannel for her own use, and the other maids iron on a different dresser.

The Housekeeper and Others

THE HOUSEKEEPER WASHES AND IRONS HER OWN SMALL things and her Mistress's. A board at Vinters has been put up for her in the mangling room, that the heat might be avoided in summer.

Housekeeper mends her Master's silk stockings, ruffles his shirts, and new collars and risbands them. The maids have generally time enough to stitch them, if they are put in hand in good time.

The chambermaid's needle work is entirely under the direction of the Governess, as it is for the young ladies and for James, but she may be taken off whenever the Housekeeper requires her assistance below. As her house work is over so early in the morning, she has all the rest of the day to work at her needle, or assist in the house when much company or a busy time makes it necessary. She must rise to wash her own things with the other maids, and iron them of an evening.

All the linen looked over in the Storeroom Monday morning, and stains taken out, etc. Housekeeper to put any stitches in Mr Whatman's muslin neckcloths that Mrs W has not mended for him.

There should be a large table in the Storeroom for the maids to mend sheets or anything that requires pressing, for, although the Housekeeper sets out all this kind of work, yet, unless it is tacked on upon a flat surface, it will seldom lay smooth, and occasions in the end more work by tearing out.

The Laundrymaid ought to stick a pin or make some other distinction upon anything that wants mending when she puts it in the basket, or if a string is wanting, etc. If any muslin goes to the wash with a large tear, it should be ruff dryed.

To keep up the Bedchamber fires when fresh coals are put on, it is sufficient to press down the fire and throw the cinders up over the fresh coals, but not to stir up the fire first unless it is likely to be going out. A clear fire only requires pressing down. No fire should ever be put out with water. It makes the dust fly all over the room, and gives much trouble in cleaning the bars. The persons themselves are covered with blacks, and the cast iron back will be spoilt by cracking. This dirty trick of pouring water on the fire will also occasion the cast iron at the back of the grate to split.

All the servants may go to bed early, and some necessarily must, if they do their duty in the morning.

On Monday night the Housemaid need not sit up to warm the bed for her Master, as she is expected to rise very early the next morning to wash. The Housekeeper can do it while her Mistress is undressing.

The Housekeeper and Others

The Housekeeper and Butler should see all fires and candles out before they go to bed.

The first thing a Housekeeper should teach a new servant is to carry her candle upright. The next is those general directions that belong to *her* place in *particular*, such as not setting the brooms and brushes where they will make a mark, and all those common directions.

A Housekeeper by practise must acquire so quick an eye that, if she comes occasionally into a room that is cleaning, she must see at once if it is going on properly.

One of the most useful common directions next to carrying a candle upright is that of putting away chairs, tables, or anything that goes next a wall, with a hand behind it. For want of this trifling attention great pieces are frequently knocked out of the stucco, and the backs of the chairs, if bending, leave a mark on the wall.

The beds always well shook.

If the under servants could be depended on for doing all their business *according to the instructions that could be given them*, the eye of a Housekeeper would not be necessary to keep every thing going on in its proper way. But this is never to be expected, and as the mistress of a large family can neither afford the time, nor even have it in her power, to see what her servants are about, she must depend upon the Housekeeper to see all her orders enforced and every rule kept up. For rules are not laid down unnecessarily and, when neglected, the inconvenience is felt in future, tho perhaps not immediately, and when the mischief has crept in, it is too late to go back again to a preventive rule. At least experience proves it to be *very* difficult.

The Dairymaid should milk her cows at the same hour nearly night and morning, and, after milking the last, take the little wooden bowl to strip the cows all round. In hot weather the milk must not be poured into the pans till it is cold, and sometimes it is necessary to put some cold pump water into the pans to make the cream throw up well.

All the particular rules in a family respecting the work of each servant, and also the general rules, should be inforced by the Housekeeper by making it inconvenient to the individuals to neglect them, which prevents all disputes, as well as complaints on either side, for if it becomes more trouble to do a thing improperly, the *temptation* of doing so ceases.

Every new servant must be very particularly attended to in doing her business till she is got into the way of the family. It is easier to *prevent* a bad method of doing the work than to alter it afterwards.

Plenty of sugar should always be kept ready broke[1] in the deep sugar drawers in the Closet Storeroom. There is one for spice, one for moist sugar, and two for lump sugar. The pieces should be as square as possible, and rather small. The sugar that is powdered to fill the silver castor should be kept in a bason in one of the drawers to prevent any insects getting into it, and be powdered *fine* in the mortar and kept ready for use. Currants and raisins should be kept in a moister place, as in the deep drawers in the little cupboard opposite the Storeroom. Rice should be ground at leizure times, and kept for use. Currant also dried a little before wanted are convenient, as they should be used quite dry.

A tub is to stand in a corner of the Storeroom with coals which may be put on with a shovel. And the small wooden coal tub which belongs to the Schoolroom should not be brought downstairs, but stand in the passage close to the Schoolroom.

Any linen that is become yellow by laying by should be used once in the spring or summer when the cloaths can be dried out of doors. If the weather proves unfavorable,

---

[1] Refined sugar was then generally marketed in conical loaves.

rough dry them, and keep them to another wash, then dip them in water and hang them out again.

The pillow bears in constant use should not have any strings because, if they have, it is difficult to get the maids to tack them and, if they are not tacked, they wear much sooner.

A servant is not to go out without asking leave. Neither is she to expect to have leave every Sunday that it is her turn to go to Church. Such a custom would be the means of laying the servants under constant and frequent obligations to their friends and acquaintances, and make the leave of going out no favor at all.

[From a loose leaf at some time detached from the Book]

Mrs Whatman pays all her house bills weekly, including the Butcher's bills, and candles and flour when they are brought in. But soap, wax candles and grocery come down from London and are paid for by draft by Mr Whatman.

Mr Whatman wishes all his servants to understand that he always pays his own bills, and has always laid down a rule of never sending a message through a servant to order in his bills on any pretence whatever, neither at Xmas nor at any other time of the year, and if a tradesman should be remiss in not sending in his bill in the course of a twelvemonth, Mr Whatman will take charge of reminding him. To enforce these rules that relate to bills Mrs Whatman will.

[Here the leaf ends abruptly the bottom of the page having been cut off]

Extracts from Letters
1798–1800

To William Balston   *15 Dec* 1798

In regard to the watch and money you met with, it was
certainly neglectful in me not to have apprised you of their
being purposely so disposed. It was the mode in which Mr
W always kept anything of value, and he never would have
the closet dusted, or even the cobwebs disturbed, as he
thought it much safer in the case of thieves: the guineas in
that bag he would never be without, ever since the miseries
which broke out in France and our being so near a revolu-
tion, and he hung it behind the case where he thought it
most likely to escape search. That guinea with a memoran-
dum about Mr Lloyd was relative to a bet he (Mr W) had
won and wished to contrive to lose back again. . . .

I dont know how we shall be able to explain to James the

finding of the philosophical index, for I pledged myself to him that Davis would keep her word in never again taking down the books to dust after I had told her of the mischief that insued the last time, and I requested her never to do it again, only to use a wing to the books as they stand. I never saw her poor late master so angry as once that they had taken the busts down and dusted them, and indeed with reason, as he always begd they might be left alone, and the books too. But be cautious what you say, because she means well, and it is a very common fault not to give a master or a mistress credit for any positive order which it requires reflexion to see the consequence of.

To the same   *13 April* 1799

I enclose a bit of callico. I should like to know what opinion the maids have of it. It is a finer one than I should have given them, but it is *so pretty* that if they *fell in love* with it as I did, I should be tempted to take it. Davis could easily discover.

To the same   *14 August* 1799

I shall beg Davis to have my Dressingroom carpet shook out, and to see the moths do not get into it. I think she had better have the carpets in the Library and the Eating Parlour turned on the wrong side. It gets out the dust much better than beating them, and let them remain so after we come back a little while. But above all I beg the floors of those two rooms may not be wetted while I am absent, at least not till I mention it.

To Mrs Hester Davis   *17 Sept* 1799

I think now that you will hardly see Laetitia's little girl again, as they propose merely coming down to the christening. Therefore I do not see any objection to cleaning up below stairs. And I shall thank you to be careful that the carpets do not get any wet when they scower the rooms, for the Library carpet has suffered sadly, as the greens always run if not dried immediately, and if by *any accident* a little wet should get to them, to have them directly unfolded and wiped.

I should be glad to have the boards dry rubbed a great many times, till they are in that state under the windows that a little dry dirt will come off without wetting. For the men are so very apt to bring in sand with their shoes that there is no other way of keeping the boards decent, unless they are often wet, which has already very much spoilt their colour, and given them a white look. This is one of the inconveniences of changing housemaids often, because it is some time before one can make them understand these kind of things. The Hall should also be well dry rubbed several times, and the best stair case with the hand brush and sand.

I hope Sally takes care of the mahogany balustrade, and is careful to take off all fresh spots on the steel round the fire place: the flies are very apt to make spots in the summer.

To William Balston   *26 Oct* 1799

I wish the carpets to remain on the wrong side, the intention of putting them so being that the walking on them should beat out the dust.

To the same   *27 June* 1800

This is glorious weather for hay making, but sadly *hot* for being in London. I hope the sun is kept from the pictures and furniture. The blinds will not always exclude it. I am often obliged to shut the shudders. Remind them of the blinds in the Hall: they sd be down by the middle of the day.

The following instructions are found in a draft, partly in Susanna's handwriting and partly in her son's, written on paper watermarked 1807. They may well belong to 1811 when Susanna was handing over Vinters to James on his marriage to her niece, Elizabeth Susanna Gaussen.

Extracts from Letters

In James's handwriting

BUTLER

Always to keep the key of the ale, to draw it himself, and never allow any other to go down for him. (N.B. to make it a fault in any one who does at the Butler's request.)

To preside and deliver out the ale himself, and not to put the Coachman or other servant in his place.

To keep the allowance for such persons whose work has prevented them coming to dinner at the usual time.

A Cellar Book to be kept by the Butler. He ought to mention at dinner whenever it is a fresh tap.

Cellar locked up at night, and the key taken upstairs by the Butler.

To receive candles from the Housekeeper, and not to allow the Footmen to ask for them.

To go behind the carriage. To wear a livery. To carry and bring back his parcels and linen from the wash.

Never to take any friend or stranger into the Pantry.

Care of the key of the plate.

Do.   do.   of bottle rack.

To lock the cellar door at night and take the key upstairs and not to allow it to be opened until he comes down in the morning.

ALLOWANCE TO THE SERVANTS

Ale. 1 pint to the men, and ½ a pint to the maids per day. Small beer. As much as they chuse.

N.B. Any servant who absents himself from dinner must of course lose his ale, but if absent about his Master's business, the Butler must keep it for him.

CHEESE

No cheese allowed after a meal. When cheese is given, it should be for a meal and in lieu of meat, when it comes as cheap as anything else.

The Housekeeping Book

SERVANTS
Always to carry their own parcels etc. to and from Maidstone, and not to have them brought over by tradesmen or friends to the House.

WASHING
The night preceding a light must be left burning all night for the maids to get up by. To take care that it is put in a safe place and without risk of fire.

Not to leave the linen in the drying ground at night, as it has been stolen.

WASHING SHEEP
Beginning of June to July, according to the season. Hollands for the men in the water.

SHEARING
Odd man to dine at noon with the shearers, and not afterwards, in order that he may *always* be with them.

HAYSTACK
See that the stack is drawn in soon enough that the top may have a sufficient slope. Hence, to notice that when the stack is set out it is not too large for the probable quantity of hay.

In Susanna's handwriting

KITCHEN
No kitchen stuff allowed on any account but what is not wanted to be sold.

Housekeeper always to see that the men's breakfasts are well sent up and good.

GUTTERS
Cleaned out once a year. Cut the ivy round them and the window frames. Gutters, when cleaned out, to be examined if in want of pitch or paint.

Gutters in the Court – the iron roofs not to be swept with a hard broom on account of rubbing of the paint.

Biographical Afterword
by
Thomas Balston

Tragedy struck the sunny, well-regulated world of Vinters
in 1790. James, aged only forty-eight, suffered a severe
paralytic stroke, which reduced him to an invalid for the
rest of the year and permanently affected his health and
spirits. Although he remained active in the paper-making
business for three more years, in 1793, to the surprise of
Susanna and William Balston, who had been his chief assistant for many years, he sold his two mills to the brothers
Hollingworth for £20,000. The sale was completed in
October 1794, and Whatman spent the next few years in
improving the Vinters estates and supervising his investments. Except for three months in 1796 when he was again
incapacitated, he had no serious illness, and as late as May
1797 he paid Humphry Repton 50 guineas for 'Plans and
Surveys of Vinters', one of Repton's characteristic notebooks with many coloured drawings of the estate super-
imposed by movable flaps which show the alterations he
recommended. [Sadly no trace of this note-book survives].
In March 1798 he went to London to make his Will, return-
ing on the 10th. On the morning of the 17th he made the
last entry in his accounts, and later that day he died,
aged 56.

By his will, Whatman left Vinters to Susanna for her life,
and also about half his investments absolutely, 'trusting to
the experience I have had of her great worth and discretion

that they will not be impaired'. For thirteen more years she made Vinters her headquarters. Camilla had married a neighbouring baronet, Sir Charles Style of Wateringbury, in 1794, and, two months before her father's death, Laetitia married Susanna's cousin, Samuel Bosanquet. Balston, by then a partner of the Hollingworth Brothers' firm and Chairman of the Master Paper Makers, moved to Poll Mill, but was still near enough to be consulted almost daily about her affairs, or by weekly letters when she was away. Only James, then twenty-one and a Fellow Commoner of Trinity College, Cambridge, was much with her, but he was in an almost desperate state of hypochondria. Much of the next two years Susanna spent with him at Shoreham, where it was hoped he would benefit by bathing, and during these absences Susanna wrote the letters to Balston and Hester Davies. In 1811, James married Susanna's niece, Elizabeth Gaussen, and Susanna handed over the estate to him, and went to live at Northaw Cottage, Hertfordshire. Later she moved to Baker Street, where she died on November 29th, 1814, aged seventy-six.

Her later years were much troubled by ill-health, by disasters among her many relations, and by a tiresome lawsuit with an eminent physician, Sir Charles Addis. Quite unaware that two hundred years after it was written, her practical little guide would reach a far wider audience than she had ever intended, she resigned herself contentedly to the bitter blows fate was dealing her. As this letter to William Balston shows, she retained that unquestioning [not to say Panglossian] acceptance of the actual conditions of life which is apparent throughout her book.

My trust in providence is unbounded. I have not the most distant doubt that everything is working together for the best ultimately, although it is very possible that for wise reasons the issue in the world may not be what we short-sighted mortals should esteem favourable.